Spotter's Guide to
INDOOR PLANTS

Ann Bonar

Illustrated by Will Giles & Dee McLean

with additional illustrations by
Andy Martin

Contents

Edited by
Helen Gilks

Series editor
Bridget Gibbs

First published in 1980 by
Usborne Publishing Limited,
20 Garrick Street, London WC2

Published in Australia by Rigby
Publishing Ltd, Adelaide, Sydney,
Melbourne, Brisbane.

Printed and bound in Great Britain by
Morrison & Gibb Ltd, London and Edinburgh

How to use this book

This book will help you to identify and care for some of the most popular indoor plants.

The main part of the book is divided into five sections: plants kept for their attractive leaves (grouped by leaf colour), flowering plants, plants which bear fruit, vase plants, and cacti and other fleshy plants. Remember that though the plants in the flowering section are shown with flowers of one colour, you may see the same plant with flowers of a different colour. You may also spot a flowering plant when it has no flowers, so try looking in the flowering section if you cannot find a plant in the leaf section.

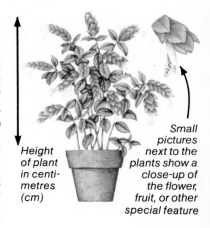

Height of plant in centimetres (cm)

Small pictures next to the plants show a close-up of the flower, fruit, or other special feature

Caring for indoor plants

Pages 49-51 tell you how to care for plants and how to provide them with good growing conditions. At the beginning of each section, such as the one on flowering plants, you will find a few general notes on how to keep those particular plants.

The descriptions next to each illustration tell you any additional points you need to know. They give the minimum temperature (MT) that the plant can survive and they also tell you the best kind of light for the plant (see page 51 for more about light). If no instructions for watering are given in the descriptions, you should water the compost when it is dry and crumbly as described on page 49.

Most plants need a certain amount of humidity and may benefit from being misted (sprayed), especially if their leaves start to look dried up. You can read more about this on page 50.

Measurements

The plants are not drawn exactly to scale, but the description gives the average height to which a plant will grow indoors. For some plants, the length of the leaf is given. Leaves are measured from the tip to the point where they join the stalk.

Names of plants

If a plant has an English name, it is given in the description. If it does not, the scientific name, in Latin, is used. Cultivar names (see page 5) are written in single inverted commas.

Scorecard and tick circle

Beside each description is a small blank circle; when you spot a plant, make a tick in the circle. At the back of the book is a scorecard that gives you a score for every plant in the book. A common plant scores 5 and a rare one 25 points.

Describing plants

Leaf shapes
Leaves can be simple or made up of several leaflets. They can also be many different shapes. To make it easier to identify plants, each shape has been given a special term. The terms used to describe leaves in this book are illustrated below.

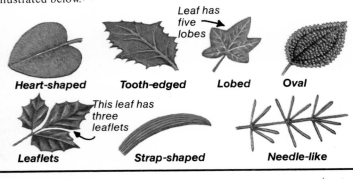

Leaf has five lobes →

Heart-shaped   **Tooth-edged**   **Lobed**   **Oval**

This leaf has three leaflets →

Leaflets   **Strap-shaped**   **Needle-like**

Some useful words

Variegated leaf ▶
A green leaf that is edged, striped or spotted with cream, white or yellow.

Rosette ▶
A cluster of leaves without stems, usually growing straight out of the ground.

◀ Spike
An unbranched stem that has flowers arranged along it. The flowers usually have very short stalks.

◀ Bract
A leaf-like structure, often brightly coloured, which grows near the flowers of some plants.

Rib ▶
A ridge on the body of a cactus
Spine ▶
A sharp, thorn-like growth on cacti and other fleshy plants.

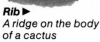

Spines →
Rib →

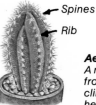

Aerial root ▶
A root that grows from the stem of a climbing plant and helps to support it.

Aerial root →

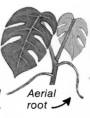

What are indoor plants?

Most of our indoor plants grow wild in hot countries. If you were to visit South America, for example, you would see many of the plants shown in this book growing wild in forests, mountains or deserts. The plants would often be much larger than when grown indoors. In each habitat there would be different plants specially adapted to the conditions of the area. A plant will grow best indoors if given conditions similar to those that it has in the wild.

Ferns, for example, grow in forests where the air is very damp and there is not much sunlight. They grow best indoors if kept moist and in shade.

Ferns grow on the ground in jungles and forests

◄ Cacti

Cacti grow in desert conditions where there is little rain and hot dry weather. They have thick stems that store water for periods when there is no rain, and, in most cases, their leaves have been reduced to spines, so there is little surface area from which water can be lost. Cacti grow best indoors in a sunny position with little watering and dry air.

Cultivars and hybrids ►

Some indoor plants have been specially selected by nurserymen because they are stronger or more beautiful varieties of the original plant. These are called cultivars. The cultivar name is written in inverted commas after the name of the plant from which it was developed. Other plants, especially flowering ones, are grown from seed produced by crossing male and female flowers of closely related plants. These are called hybrids.

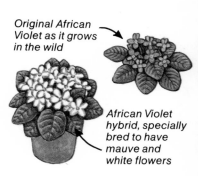

Original African Violet as it grows in the wild

African Violet hybrid, specially bred to have mauve and white flowers

Green-leaved plants

The plants on pages 6-13 are grown for their attractive leaves; many of them never flower indoors. Most of them need shade or indirect light.

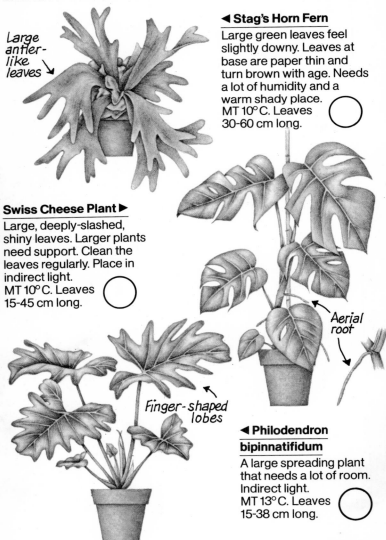

Large antler-like leaves

◄ Stag's Horn Fern

Large green leaves feel slightly downy. Leaves at base are paper thin and turn brown with age. Needs a lot of humidity and a warm shady place. MT 10° C. Leaves 30-60 cm long.

Swiss Cheese Plant ►

Large, deeply-slashed, shiny leaves. Larger plants need support. Clean the leaves regularly. Place in indirect light. MT 10° C. Leaves 15-45 cm long.

Aerial root

Finger-shaped lobes

◄ Philodendron bipinnatifidum

A large spreading plant that needs a lot of room. Indirect light. MT 13° C. Leaves 15-38 cm long.

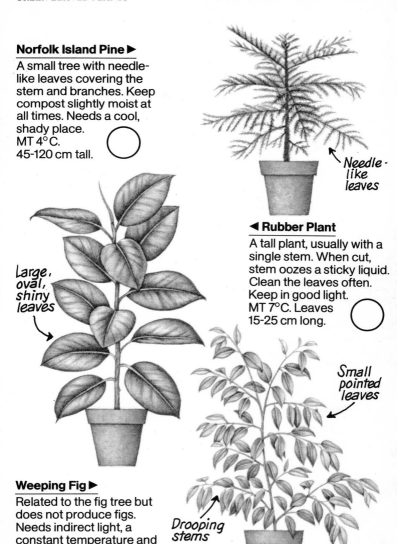

Norfolk Island Pine ▶

A small tree with needle-like leaves covering the stem and branches. Keep compost slightly moist at all times. Needs a cool, shady place.
MT 4°C.
45-120 cm tall.

Needle-like leaves

◀ Rubber Plant

A tall plant, usually with a single stem. When cut, stem oozes a sticky liquid. Clean the leaves often. Keep in good light.
MT 7°C. Leaves 15-25 cm long.

Large, oval, shiny leaves

Small pointed leaves

Weeping Fig ▶

Related to the fig tree but does not produce figs. Needs indirect light, a constant temperature and a lot of humidity.
MT 7°C.
60-120 cm tall.

Drooping stems

Kangaroo Vine ▶

A fast-growing, climbing plant with toothed leaves. Needs a cool, shady place; leaves turn yellow if plant is in bright light. Provide support. MT 7°C. Leaves 4-8 cm long.

Tendrils help plant to climb

Toothed leaves

Each leaf has three leaflets

◀ Rhoicissus 'Ellen Danica'

This climbing plant is a cultivar of the Grape Ivy. Each leaf has three, lobed leaflets. Needs shade and cool conditions. Provide support. MT 7°C. Leaves 5-17 cm long.

Grape Ivy ▶

Toothed, diamond-shaped leaflets grow in groups of three. Stem and undersides of leaves are hairy. Tendrils help support plant as it climbs. Needs cool and shade. MT 7°C. Leaves 5-17 cm long.

Asparagus sprengeri ▶

This plant has long, trailing stems with tiny needle-like leaves. It is related to the vegetable, asparagus. Keep compost slightly moist at all times. Needs a cool, shady place.
MT 4°C.
30-60 cm tall.

Needle-like leaves grouped in fives

Heart-shaped leaves

◀ Sweetheart Vine

A trailing or climbing plant with thick, soft stems. Not related to the grape-producing vine. Keep in a cool, shady place and take care not to over-water in winter.
MT 7°C. Leaves 15-30 cm long.

Arrow-leaved Ivy ▶

Undersides of stems have short aerial roots for climbing, but plant may also trail. Each leaf has three large lobes and two smaller ones. Keep in a cool shady place.
MT 2°C. Leaves 2.5-5 cm long.

Central lobe is longer than others

9

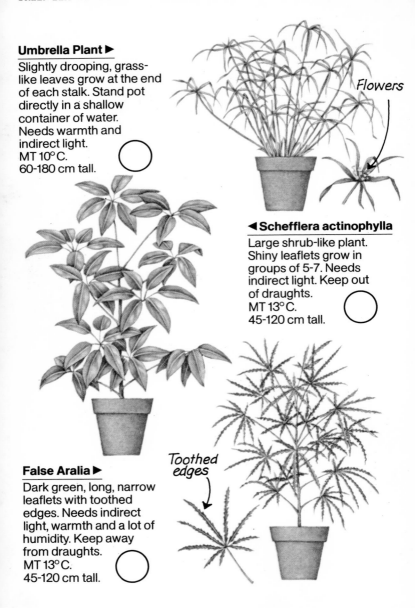

Umbrella Plant ▶

Slightly drooping, grass-like leaves grow at the end of each stalk. Stand pot directly in a shallow container of water. Needs warmth and indirect light.
MT 10°C.
60-180 cm tall.

Flowers

◀ Schefflera actinophylla

Large shrub-like plant. Shiny leaflets grow in groups of 5-7. Needs indirect light. Keep out of draughts.
MT 13°C.
45-120 cm tall.

False Aralia ▶

Dark green, long, narrow leaflets with toothed edges. Needs indirect light, warmth and a lot of humidity. Keep away from draughts.
MT 13°C.
45-120 cm tall.

Toothed edges

10

Young leaves grow
from centre
of stem

Long,
narrow
leaflets

◀ Parlour Palm
New leaves are at first
sheathed, then expand into
feathery palm leaves. Keep
in indirect light. Must have
soft water or else leaves
turn brown.
MT 10°C.
60-120 cm tall.

Kentia Palm ▶
Long, slender leaf stems
with drooping leaflets
arranged in a fan shape.
Like Parlour Palm, needs
soft water and indirect
light.
MT 10°C.
180 cm tall.

Stiff
leaflets

◀ Date Palm
Stiff, upright leaflets grow
close together on leaf
stems. Needs good light
and soft water. Watch for
scale insects.
MT 4°C.
90-180 cm tall.

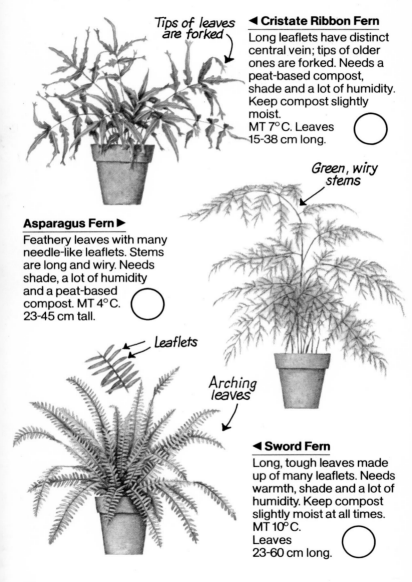

Tips of leaves are forked

◀ Cristate Ribbon Fern

Long leaflets have distinct central vein; tips of older ones are forked. Needs a peat-based compost, shade and a lot of humidity. Keep compost slightly moist.
MT 7°C. Leaves 15-38 cm long.

Green, wiry stems

Asparagus Fern ▶

Feathery leaves with many needle-like leaflets. Stems are long and wiry. Needs shade, a lot of humidity and a peat-based compost. MT 4°C. 23-45 cm tall.

Leaflets

Arching leaves

◀ Sword Fern

Long, tough leaves made up of many leaflets. Needs warmth, shade and a lot of humidity. Keep compost slightly moist at all times.
MT 10°C.
Leaves 23-60 cm long.

Flower spikes appear in spring

Heart-shaped leaves

◀ Peperomia caperata

Plant has ridged, rounded leaves on short stems. Tiny white flowers grow on red stems in spring. Needs warmth, good light and plenty of humidity. MT 13°C. 15-30 cm tall.

Arching black stems

Maidenhair Fern ▶

Delicate-looking plant with feathery leaves and black wiry stems. Keep in shade; provide a lot of humidity. MT 10°C. 30-38 cm tall.

New plant

◀ Piggy-back Plant

Tiny new plants grow from top side of leaves where they join the leaf stalks. Small green-brown flowers appear in summer. Does well in light or shade. Easy to grow. MT 4°C. 20-30 cm tall.

13

Plants with coloured leaves

Most of the plants on pages 14-27 do not flower indoors and are kept for their coloured, or partly coloured, leaves. In general, they need more light than plants with leaves that are completely green.

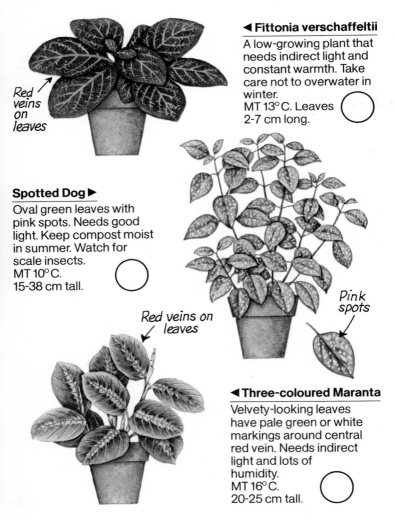

Red veins on leaves

◄ Fittonia verschaffeltii
A low-growing plant that needs indirect light and constant warmth. Take care not to overwater in winter.
MT 13°C. Leaves 2-7 cm long.

Spotted Dog ►
Oval green leaves with pink spots. Needs good light. Keep compost moist in summer. Watch for scale insects.
MT 10°C.
15-38 cm tall.

Pink spots

Red veins on leaves

◄ Three-coloured Maranta
Velvety-looking leaves have pale green or white markings around central red vein. Needs indirect light and lots of humidity.
MT 16°C.
20-25 cm tall.

Cordyline ▶

Long green leaves are streaked with red and branch off from a single stem. Needs good light and a lot of humidity.
MT 10°C.
60-75 cm tall.

Long, pointed leaves

Narrow, arching leaves

◀ Three-coloured
Dracaena

Tall plant with woody central stem and narrow leaves edged with cream and pink. Needs good light and constant warmth. MT 16°C.
120-150 cm tall.

Caladium ▶

Large, heart-shaped leaves are like paper tissue. Needs warmth, indirect light and plenty of humidity. Keep compost moist.
MT 18°C.
60-120 cm tall.

Thin, papery leaves

15

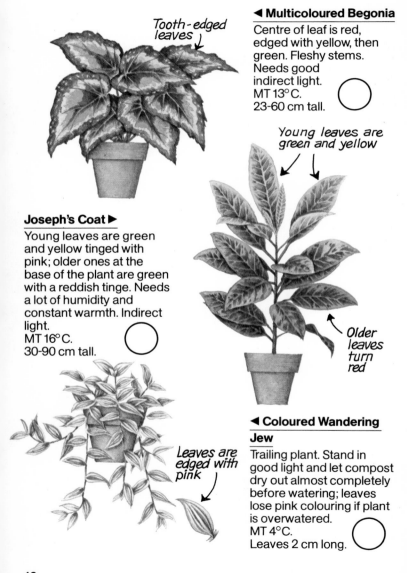

Tooth-edged leaves

◀ Multicoloured Begonia

Centre of leaf is red, edged with yellow, then green. Fleshy stems. Needs good indirect light.
MT 13°C.
23-60 cm tall.

Young leaves are green and yellow

Joseph's Coat ▶

Young leaves are green and yellow tinged with pink; older ones at the base of the plant are green with a reddish tinge. Needs a lot of humidity and constant warmth. Indirect light.
MT 16°C.
30-90 cm tall.

Older leaves turn red

Leaves are edged with pink

◀ Coloured Wandering Jew

Trailing plant. Stand in good light and let compost dry out almost completely before watering; leaves lose pink colouring if plant is overwatered.
MT 4°C.
Leaves 2 cm long.

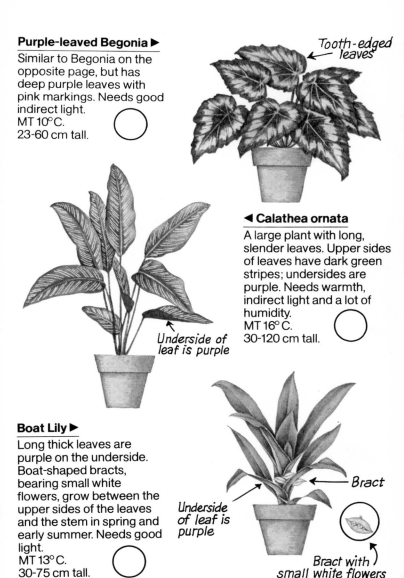

Purple-leaved Begonia ▶

Similar to Begonia on the opposite page, but has deep purple leaves with pink markings. Needs good indirect light.
MT 10°C.
23-60 cm tall.

Tooth-edged leaves

◀ Calathea ornata

A large plant with long, slender leaves. Upper sides of leaves have dark green stripes; undersides are purple. Needs warmth, indirect light and a lot of humidity.
MT 16° C.
30-120 cm tall.

Underside of leaf is purple

Boat Lily ▶

Long thick leaves are purple on the underside. Boat-shaped bracts, bearing small white flowers, grow between the upper sides of the leaves and the stem in spring and early summer. Needs good light.
MT 13°C.
30-75 cm tall.

Underside of leaf is purple

Bract

Bract with small white flowers

17

Leaves are tooth-edged

◄ Purple Passion Vine

The whole of this trailing plant is thickly covered with purple hairs. Prune stems to keep them about 30 cm long. Stand in good light and never get leaves wet.
MT 10°C. Leaves 6 cm long.

Zebrina pendula ►

Thick leaves are striped silver-grey and green, and are tinged with purple on upper side; underside is purple. Needs good light.
MT 10°C.
Leaves 5 cm long.

Underside

Upper side of leaf

Stems are slightly hairy

Tiny mauve flowers

◄ Purple Heart

A trailing plant with long, narrow leaves. The whole plant turns deep purple if kept in a good light.
MT 13°C.
Leaves 9 cm long.

18

Iron Cross Begonia ▶

A bushy plant with deeply ridged, light green leaves that have a brown cross on the upper side. Needs good indirect light.
MT 10°C.
20-30 cm tall.

Dark cross on leaves

Leaves have a lop-sided point

Oval-shaped leaves with brown veins

◀ Pilea 'Moonglow'

Small bushy plant. Leaves grow in pairs and have dark brown veins in grooves between ridges. Needs indirect light. MT 10°C.
15-25 cm tall.

Leaves are rolled up when young

Prayer Plant ▶

The leaves of this plant have a pattern of brown blotches on the upper surface and stand erect at night. Needs good indirect light and a lot of humidity.
MT 10°C.
15-30 cm tall.

Plants with variegated leaves

Chinese Evergreen ▶

Long, oval, shiny leaves have "V"-shaped bands of yellow colouring. Needs indirect light and a lot of humidity.
MT 10°C.
30-60 cm tall.

Large, pointed oval leaves

◀ Dumb Cane

Oval leaves are blotched with yellow on upper surface. Sap is poisonous. Needs indirect light and a lot of humidity.
MT 13°C.
30-75 cm tall.

Peperomia 'Greengold' ▶

Short thick stems and thick leaves. Keep in good light and provide a lot of humidity. Take care not to overwater in winter.
MT 10°C.
20-35 cm tall.

Rounded green leaves with yellow edges

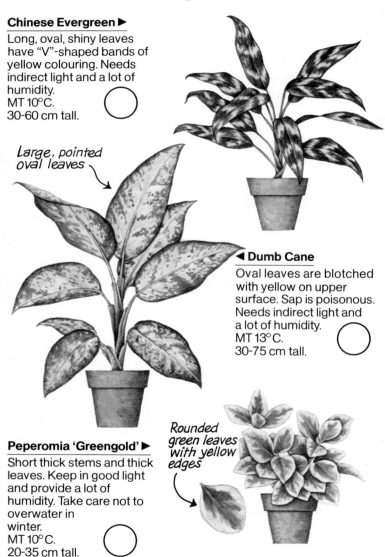

Dracaena 'Victoriae' ▶

Long, ribbon-like leaves have yellow edges and green stripes along centre. Good light. Keep out of draughts.
MT 10°C.
20-35 cm tall.

Leaves have wavy → edges

Yellow veins on leaves ↙

◀ Croton

A slow-growing plant with shiny leaves forked into three lobes. Stand in good light.
MT 16°C.
30-60 cm tall.

Edges of leaves are wavy ↙

Dracaena fragrans

massangeana ▶

Similar to Dracaena above but edges of leaves are green. Stand in good light. Keep out of draughts. MT 13°C.
30-60 cm tall.

21

Ivy 'Goldheart' ▶

A slow-growing ivy with small aerial roots on the stems which support it as it climbs. Stems are red when young. Place in good light and provide a lot of humidity.
MT 4°C. Leaves 2-7 cm long.

Lobed leaves have yellow centre

◀ Devil's Ivy

Climbing plant with fleshy stems and thick leaves. Long aerial roots grow from stems. Place in indirect light and take care not to overwater.
MT 10°C. Leaves 2-10 cm long.

Pointed, heart-shaped leaves

Ivy 'Lutzii' ▶

A small-leaved ivy with yellow and light green speckled leaves. Fairly fast growing. Keep in good light and provide pole for it to climb up.
MT 4°C.
Leaves 3 cm long.

Speckled leaves

Leaves are striped yellow and green

◀ Yellow Wandering Jew

Trailing plant with fleshy jointed stems. Pointed, oval leaves. Place in good light and keep compost slightly moist.
MT 7° C. Leaves 2.5 cm long.

Striped yellow leaves arch from centre

Spider Plant ▶

Plant puts out long stems with small white flowers and new plantlets. Easy to grow. Good light.
MT 4° C.
23-30 cm tall.

New plantlets

Leaves are edged with yellow

Pointed, oval leaves

◀ Trailing Fig

A trailing plant that grows roots at the leaf joints if the stems touch soil. Needs good light and a lot of humidity.
MT 13° C. Leaves 2-7 cm long.

Dark green leaves with white veins

◀ Snakeskin Plant

Tends to grow sideways and will root at leaf joints if stems touch compost. Closely packed leaves. Keep in indirect light and away from draughts.
MT 13°C.
Leaves 2-10 cm long.

Pilea involucrata ▶

Olive-green leaves are covered almost completely with silvery-white veins. Young leaves have a reddish tinge. Stand in indirect light.
MT 10°C.
15-23 cm tall.

Leaves grow in pairs

Young leaves are tinged red

Oval leaves with silvery patches

◀ Aluminium Plant

Upper sides of leaves have silvery patches. Pinch out tips of shoots to make the plant bushy. Needs good light and constant warmth.
MT 13°C.
30-75 cm tall.

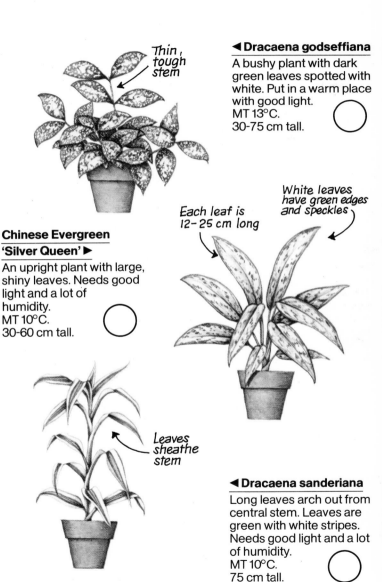

Thin, tough stem

◄ Dracaena godseffiana

A bushy plant with dark green leaves spotted with white. Put in a warm place with good light.
MT 13°C.
30-75 cm tall.

Chinese Evergreen
'Silver Queen' ►

An upright plant with large, shiny leaves. Needs good light and a lot of humidity.
MT 10°C.
30-60 cm tall.

Each leaf is 12–25 cm long

White leaves have green edges and speckles

Leaves sheathe stem

◄ Dracaena sanderiana

Long leaves arch out from central stem. Leaves are green with white stripes. Needs good light and a lot of humidity.
MT 10°C.
75 cm tall.

Green leaves with white stripes

◄ Large Wandering Jew

Similar to other Wandering Jews but leaves are larger and stems thicker. Always keep compost slightly moist. Needs good light. MT 4°C.
Leaves 4 cm long.

Variegated Canary Ivy ►

Large-leaved ivy. Small aerial roots grow on the stems. Dark green leaves with irregular creamy-white or grey edges. Needs good light and a lot of humidity.
MT 4°C. Leaves 5-12 cm long.

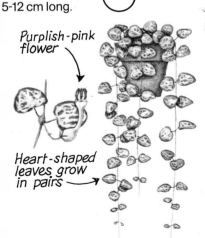

Purplish-pink flower

Heart-shaped leaves grow in pairs →

Leaves have three lobes →

◄ String of Hearts

Thread-like stems and fleshy leaves. Small flowers grow from leaf joints in summer. Keep in good light. Take care not to overwater in winter.
MT 7°C. Leaves 0.5-2 cm long.

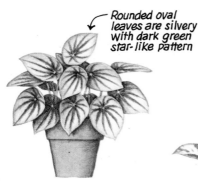

Rounded oval leaves are silvery with dark green star-like pattern

◄ Peperomia argyreia

Fleshy leaves and red stems. Place in good light away from draughts and let compost dry out before watering.
MT 10°C.
15-30 cm tall.

White Devil's Ivy ►

Trailing plant that will climb if given support. White leaves with green markings. Stand in good light.
MT 13°C. Leaves 2-10 cm long.

Taller stems produce spores

Pointed, heart-shaped leaves

◄ Variegated Ribbon Fern

Feathery leaves are mainly white on upper sides and edged with green. Tiny, seed-like reproductive structures called spores are produced on taller stems. Needs good light and plenty of humidity. MT 10°C.
30 cm tall.

27

Flowering plants

The plants on pages 28-35 are kept mainly for their showy, colourful flowers. In general, they need good light during their growing period in order to produce flowers. When you mist them, take care not to get water on the flowers. Cut off flowers as they die to encourage new ones to grow. Once a plant has finished flowering, let it rest for a few months by placing it in a shadier place and watering it less. When new growth starts, bring the plant into a better light and feed and water it regularly.

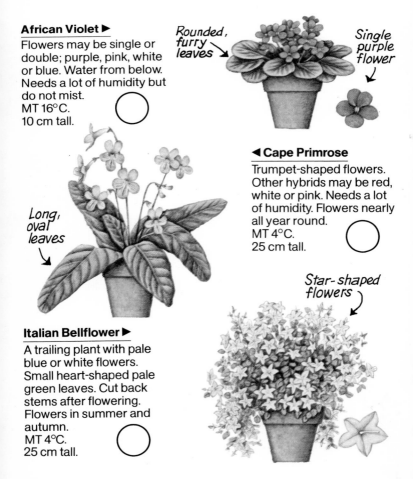

African Violet ▶
Flowers may be single or double; purple, pink, white or blue. Water from below. Needs a lot of humidity but do not mist.
MT 16°C.
10 cm tall.

Rounded, furry leaves ➘

Single purple flower ↙

◀ Cape Primrose
Trumpet-shaped flowers. Other hybrids may be red, white or pink. Needs a lot of humidity. Flowers nearly all year round.
MT 4°C.
25 cm tall.

Long, oval leaves ↘

Star-shaped flowers ⌐

Italian Bellflower ▶
A trailing plant with pale blue or white flowers. Small heart-shaped pale green leaves. Cut back stems after flowering. Flowers in summer and autumn.
MT 4°C.
25 cm tall.

Peace Lily ▶

Single white "petals" with spikes of cream-coloured flowers grow on long stems in spring, and sometimes again in autumn. Keep in indirect light. MT 16°C. Flower stems 30-40 cm.

True flowers grow as a spike

Shiny, pointed leaves

Yellow flower spike

Pointed oval leaves have white stripes

◀ Zebra Plant

Yellow flower spikes appear in winter. Water well when flowering. Needs a lot of humidity. MT 4°C. Leaves 15 cm long.

Plain green oval leaves

True flowers are white

Lollipop Plant ▶

White flowers grow on yellow spikes in summer. Keep compost moist when flowering. MT 13°C. Leaves 10 cm long.

Cyclamen ▶

Flowers are red, pink or
white and appear in winter.
Needs indirect light and
much humidity. Water from
below and keep compost
moist when in flower.
MT 16°C.
Flower stems
15-30 cm.

*Green
heart-shaped
leaves with
paler markings*

*Large,
trumpet-
shaped
flowers*

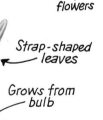

*Strap-shaped
leaves*

*Grows from
bulb*

◀ Amaryllis

Large, trumpet-shaped
flowers may be red, pink or
white. Grows from a bulb.
Feed plant while flowering
and until leaves die. Then
allow compost to dry out
completely. Start to water
four months later.
MT 10°C.
Stem 45-60 cm.

*Trumpet-shaped
flowers*

*Velvety,
oval
leaves*

Gloxinia ▶

Flowers are pink, red, blue,
purple or white; they grow
in summer and autumn.
Place in indirect light.
Water from below.
MT 10°C. Leaves
12 cm long.

30

Shrimp Plant ▶

Small white flowers hang from orange-pink spikes at ends of stems. Flowers most of the year. Cut back in late winter.
MT 13°C.
30-35 cm tall.

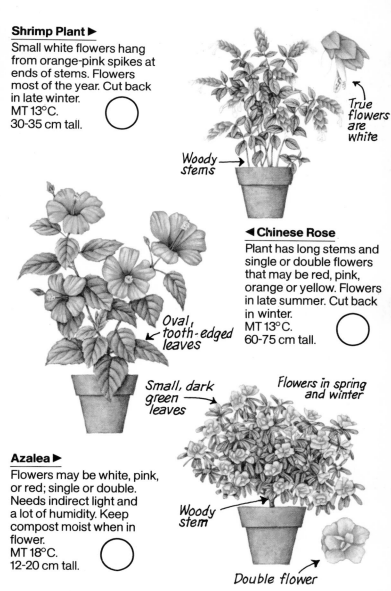

True flowers are white

Woody stems

◀ Chinese Rose

Plant has long stems and single or double flowers that may be red, pink, orange or yellow. Flowers in late summer. Cut back in winter.
MT 13°C.
60-75 cm tall.

Oval, tooth-edged leaves

Small, dark green leaves

Flowers in spring and winter

Azalea ▶

Flowers may be white, pink, or red; single or double. Needs indirect light and a lot of humidity. Keep compost moist when in flower.
MT 18°C.
12-20 cm tall.

Woody stem

Double flower

31

Busy Lizzie ▶

Thick, fleshy, transparent stems. Flowers may be any colour except blue. Needs plenty of humidity and compost should be kept moist. Cut back in late winter. Flowers from spring to winter.
MT 13°C.
30-35 cm tall.

Pointed oval leaves

Five petals

Pale pink waxy flowers

◀ Wax Flower

A slow-growing climber with clusters of star-shaped flowers. Must have plenty of humidity and soft water. Flowers in late summer.
MT 10°C. Leaves 7 cm long.

Clusters of 12-15 sweet-scented flowers

Fleshy, pointed oval leaves

Dipladenia splendens ▶

Climbing plant with shiny green leaves. Flowers grow in clusters. Needs plenty of humidity when in flower. Cut back in early spring.
MT 13°C. Leaves 12 cm long.

Yellow inside flower trumpet

Kalanchoe ▶

Shiny, fleshy leaves with toothed edges. Slender flowering stems end in clusters of tiny red or yellow flowers which appear in winter.
MT 10°C.
25 cm tall.

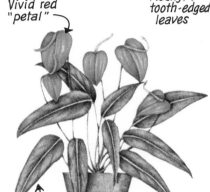

Fleshy, tooth-edged leaves

Vivid red "petal"

Long thin leaves

Flower has four petals

◀ Flamingo Flower

Flower is made up of a single red "petal" and a red spike. Needs plenty of humidity. Keep compost moist. Flowers in spring and summer.
MT 10°C. Flower stems 25 cm tall.

Begonia 'Fireglow' ▶

Plant has fleshy stems and rounded leaves with lop-sided points. Keep in indirect light. Flowers in summer and autumn.
MT 7°C.
30 cm tall.

Leaves have wavy edges

Flower has five petals

33

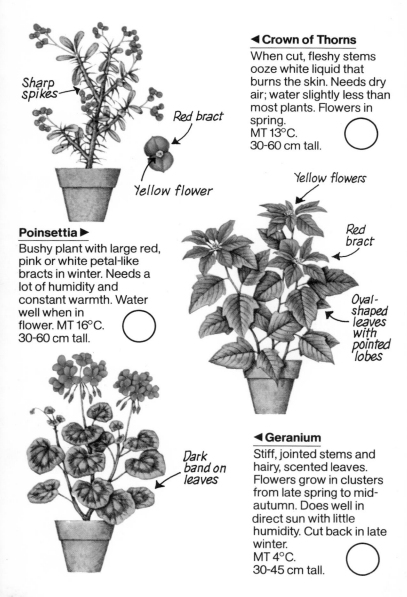

Sharp spikes

Red bract

Yellow flower

◀ Crown of Thorns
When cut, fleshy stems ooze white liquid that burns the skin. Needs dry air; water slightly less than most plants. Flowers in spring.
MT 13°C.
30-60 cm tall.

Poinsettia ▶
Bushy plant with large red, pink or white petal-like bracts in winter. Needs a lot of humidity and constant warmth. Water well when in flower. MT 16°C.
30-60 cm tall.

Yellow flowers

Red bract

Oval-shaped leaves with pointed lobes

Dark band on leaves

◀ Geranium
Stiff, jointed stems and hairy, scented leaves. Flowers grow in clusters from late spring to mid-autumn. Does well in direct sun with little humidity. Cut back in late winter.
MT 4°C.
30-45 cm tall.

Double-flowered
Begonia ▶

Large double flowers may be red, orange, white, pink or yellow. Needs indirect light. Keep compost moist when flowering and dry in winter. Flowers in summer and autumn.
MT 4°C.
30-38 cm tall.

Pointed oval leaves with toothed edges

Trumpet-shaped flowers grow in a cluster

◀ Kaffir Lily

Strap-shaped leaves grow from centre. Keep in indirect light, water normally when growing and allow compost to dry out in winter. Flowers in spring. MT 4° C.
Flower stem 30-38 cm tall.

Strap-shaped leaves

Dark green, oval waxy leaves

Clog Plant ▶

A bushy plant with shiny leaves and pouch-like, waxy flowers at each leaf joint. Needs indirect light. Cut back in February. Flowers in summer. MT 10°C.
25 cm tall.

Tiny orange flowers

35

Fruiting plants

Fruiting plants need warmth, light and moisture in order to produce fruit. During and after flowering, these plants should be kept in a good light and misted every day.

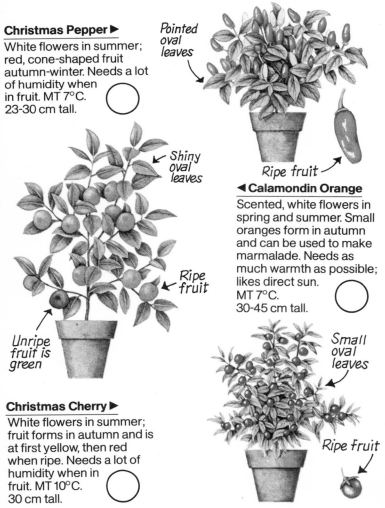

Christmas Pepper ▶

White flowers in summer; red, cone-shaped fruit autumn-winter. Needs a lot of humidity when in fruit. MT 7°C. 23-30 cm tall.

Pointed oval leaves

Ripe fruit

Shiny oval leaves

Ripe fruit

Unripe fruit is green

◀ Calamondin Orange

Scented, white flowers in spring and summer. Small oranges form in autumn and can be used to make marmalade. Needs as much warmth as possible; likes direct sun. MT 7°C. 30-45 cm tall.

Small oval leaves

Ripe fruit

Christmas Cherry ▶

White flowers in summer; fruit forms in autumn and is at first yellow, then red when ripe. Needs a lot of humidity when in fruit. MT 10°C. 30 cm tall.

Bead Plant ▶

Small, low-growing plant thickly covered with small round leaves. Tiny white flowers grow in summer; orange berries form late summer to autumn.
MT 7°C.
Leaves 0.6 cm long.

Pea-sized berries ➘

Thick rounded leaves ◀

Yellowish fruit ➘

◀ Mistletoe Fig

Thick rounded leaves. The flowers of this plant are not visible as they are enclosed in tiny capsules which grow to form the fruit in late summer and autumn.
MT 13°C.
60-75 cm tall.

Jerusalem Cherry ▶

Similar to Christmas Cherry but leaves are variegated. White flowers in summer; red, yellow or orange berries in autumn and winter.
MT 13°C.
30 cm tall.

Marble-sized berry ➘

Vase plants

Vase plants (bromeliads) generally have stiff leaves that grow in a rosette. Most of them should be watered into the "vase" formed by their leaves; the compost they grow in should also be kept just moist.

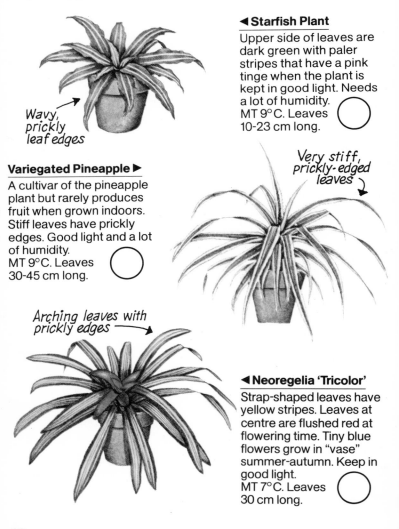

Wavy, prickly leaf edges

◀ Starfish Plant

Upper side of leaves are dark green with paler stripes that have a pink tinge when the plant is kept in good light. Needs a lot of humidity.
MT 9°C. Leaves 10-23 cm long.

Variegated Pineapple ▶

A cultivar of the pineapple plant but rarely produces fruit when grown indoors. Stiff leaves have prickly edges. Good light and a lot of humidity.
MT 9°C. Leaves 30-45 cm long.

Very stiff, prickly-edged leaves

Arching leaves with prickly edges

◀ Neoregelia 'Tricolor'

Strap-shaped leaves have yellow stripes. Leaves at centre are flushed red at flowering time. Tiny blue flowers grow in "vase" summer-autumn. Keep in good light.
MT 7°C. Leaves 30 cm long.

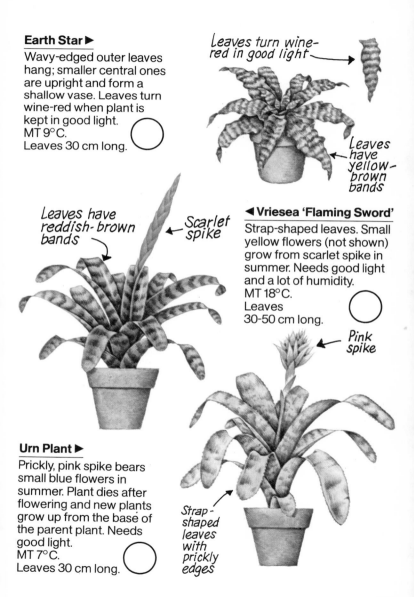

Earth Star ▶

Wavy-edged outer leaves hang; smaller central ones are upright and form a shallow vase. Leaves turn wine-red when plant is kept in good light.
MT 9°C.
Leaves 30 cm long.

Leaves turn wine-red in good light

Leaves have yellow-brown bands

Leaves have reddish-brown bands

Scarlet spike

◀ Vriesea 'Flaming Sword'

Strap-shaped leaves. Small yellow flowers (not shown) grow from scarlet spike in summer. Needs good light and a lot of humidity.
MT 18°C.
Leaves 30-50 cm long.

Pink spike

Urn Plant ▶

Prickly, pink spike bears small blue flowers in summer. Plant dies after flowering and new plants grow up from the base of the parent plant. Needs good light.
MT 7°C.
Leaves 30 cm long.

Strap-shaped leaves with prickly edges

39

Billbergia ▶

Long, narrow leaves have prickly edges. Flower heads droop from arching stems, in summer. Water compost, not "vase". Stand in indirect light. MT 10°C. Flower stems 23 cm long.

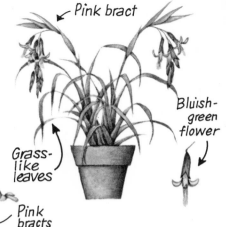

Pink bract

Bluish-green flower

Grass-like leaves

Blue flowers

Pink bracts

◀ Tillandsia cyanea

Slightly arching, stiff, grass-like leaves. Blue flowers grow between pink bracts in summer. Needs good light and a lot of humidity. MT 16°C. Leaves 30 cm long.

Red bracts

Tiny yellow flowers

Guzmania ▶

Arching, strap-shaped leaves. Yellow flowers grow between red bracts in winter. Needs indirect light and a lot of humidity. MT 13°C. Leaves 30 cm long.

Cacti and other fleshy plants

The plants on pages 41-44 have thick stems that store water. They need little watering (once a week in summer and once a month in winter is usually enough), and do well in direct sunlight. Cacti can be distinguished from other fleshy plants by the small hairy or bristly tufts, called areoles, from which spines usually grow.

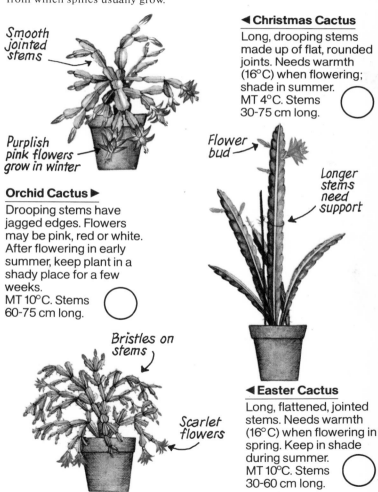

Smooth jointed stems

Purplish pink flowers grow in winter

◄ Christmas Cactus
Long, drooping stems made up of flat, rounded joints. Needs warmth (16°C) when flowering; shade in summer. MT 4°C. Stems 30-75 cm long.

Flower bud

Longer stems need support

Orchid Cactus ►
Drooping stems have jagged edges. Flowers may be pink, red or white. After flowering in early summer, keep plant in a shady place for a few weeks. MT 10°C. Stems 60-75 cm long.

Bristles on stems

Scarlet flowers

◄ Easter Cactus
Long, flattened, jointed stems. Needs warmth (16°C) when flowering in spring. Keep in shade during summer. MT 10°C. Stems 30-60 cm long.

Brown spines

Ribs

◀ Column Cactus

Cactus with a single stem. Pale brown spines grow along ribs. New plants sometimes grow from base. Slow-growing. MT 7°C. Height 45 cm or more.

Old Man Cactus ▶

A slow-growing, tall cactus covered in long, wavy hairs. Mist occasionally in summer. Keep away from draughts. MT 16°C. 30-60 cm tall.

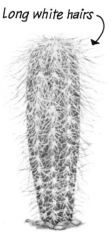

Long white hairs

White spines grow along ribs

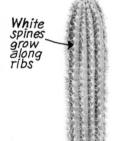

◀ Cleistocactus strausii

Fleshy stem has shallow ribs and is covered with tufts of white spines and hairs. MT 4°C. 30-60 cm tall.

Prickly Pear ▶

Made up of flat, rounded segments covered with tufts of white spines. Sometimes produces flowers. MT 7°C. 10-30 cm tall.

Flattened stem segments

Tufts of white bristles

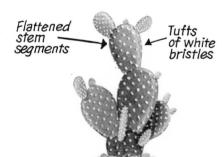

Peanut Cactus ▶

A small cactus that has many short, fat, rounded stems covered with tiny, hair-like spines. Flowers May-June.
MT 4°C.
5-10 cm tall.

Scarlet flowers close up at night

3 CM tall

Green cactus provides Ruby Ball with food

◀ Gymnocalycium 'Ruby Ball'

Small, round, red cactus that cannot make its own food. Can live only if grafted onto a green cactus that provides it with food.
MT 8°C.
3 cm tall.

Mammillaria ▶

Rounded cactus with many hairs and spines. May have red or yellow flowers. Sometimes forms red berries after a hot summer.
MT 4°C.
7-10 cm tall.

Flowers grow in a ring around top of plant

Each Living Stone is made up of two segments

◀ Living Stones

A fleshy plant made up of two thick leaves. May be patterned with grey, brown or white. Yellow or white flowers in mid-summer.
MT 4°C.
2.5 cm tall.

◄ Mother-in-law's Tongue

Stiff leaves have dark and light green bands with yellow edges. Leaves rot if compost is too wet or if temperature too low. MT 10°C. 30-60 cm tall.

Partridge-breasted Aloe ►

A rosette of upright, overlapping leaves with pointed tips. Flowers on a spike in late spring. MT 4°C. Flower stem 25 cm tall.

Red flowers

Thick fleshy leaves

V-shaped bands

Rosette of fleshy leaves

◄ Golden Bird's Nest

A low-growing fleshy plant with pointed leaves. Leaves are yellow with central green stripe. MT 4°C. Leaves 15 cm long.

Houseleek ►

Rosette of fleshy, green leaves that have brown tips. Flowers grow in clusters at the end of a long stem in summer. MT 4°C. Rosette 7 cm across.

Pink, star-shaped flowers

Insect-eating plants

Plants make most of their food from sunlight and air, using the green-coloured substance in their leaves called chlorophyll. They also obtain food, especially minerals, from the soil they grow in. Some plants also feed by trapping and digesting insects. They do this to obtain the nitrogen which is missing from the soil they grow in.

The insect-eating plants shown on this page should be kept in a warm sunny place and need to be grown in a mixture of coarse sand and moss peat. This should be kept moist at all times in summer; the best way to make sure of this is to keep the plant pot standing in a saucer of water. In winter, when the plants are not growing, the mixture should be kept just slightly moist.

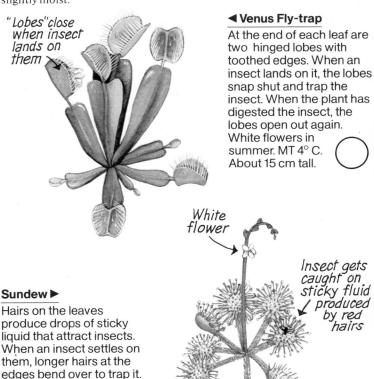

"Lobes" close when insect lands on them

◄ Venus Fly-trap

At the end of each leaf are two hinged lobes with toothed edges. When an insect lands on it, the lobes snap shut and trap the insect. When the plant has digested the insect, the lobes open out again. White flowers in summer. MT 4° C. About 15 cm tall.

White flower

Insect gets caught on sticky fluid produced by red hairs

Sundew ►

Hairs on the leaves produce drops of sticky liquid that attract insects. When an insect settles on them, longer hairs at the edges bend over to trap it. Flowers in summer. MT 4°C. Flower stem 10 cm tall.

Growing indoor bulbs

Pots of flowering bulbs look colourful around the house in winter and make good presents. You can buy Hyacinth, Daffodil and Crocus bulbs at most shops that stock garden equipment. If you want them to flower in early winter, you must buy specially treated bulbs in late summer.

Hyacinths

Do not completely cover the bulb with compost

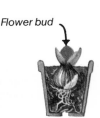

Flower bud

Spike of flowers

For each bulb, you will need a pot about 12 centimetres across. Half fill it with compost and put a bulb in the centre, then put more compost around the bulb. Water the compost and place the pot in a dark, cool place (4°-7°C) for 8 to 10 weeks. Check occasionally to see that the compost has not dried out. When the flower bud is about 2.5 cm high, bring the pot out into the light. As it grows, move it into a warmer and lighter place and water regularly. Do not hurry it with too much light or warmth too soon, or it will grow long leaves and a short flower stem.

Crocuses and Daffodils

CROCUSES

DAFFODILS

Crocus and Daffodil bulbs should be treated in the same way as Hyacinths. You can grow several bulbs together in the same pot. When the bulbs have finished flowering, you can plant them in your garden. Cut off the dead flowers but allow the leaves to wither naturally. The bulb will grow leaves the next spring but may not produce a flower until the year after.

Miniature gardens

You may like to design and plant a miniature garden. You can use all kinds of small plants and any kind of shallow container such as a plastic seed tray, a soup plate or even a saucer. It is a good idea to make a drawing on paper first, or to arrange the plants and any decorations you are using in an area the size of the container, before you plant them.

Desert garden

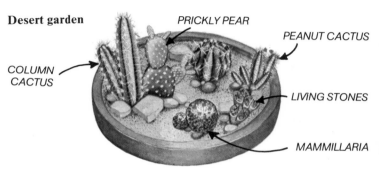

COLUMN CACTUS

PRICKLY PEAR

PEANUT CACTUS

LIVING STONES

MAMMILLARIA

To make a desert garden use very sandy compost and sprinkle a layer of sand over the surface. Add some small stones, then plant a few small cactus plants like the ones shown in the picture. Keep the cacti in a warm, sunny place and do not water them too often.

Japanese garden

SUGAR ALMOND

SPIDER PLANT

MIND YOUR OWN BUSINESS

CROWN OF THORNS

AFRICAN VIOLET

Mirror

WANDERING JEW

Moss

To make a Japanese garden, first place some small pebbles along the bottom of the container. Then put in a layer of compost and plant some plants, like the ones shown in the picture. You could make a pool with a small pot sunk into the compost, or just use a small mirror. Place some moss on the compost between the plants to give the impression of grass and use some gravel chippings for paving stones.

How to make a bromeliad tree

Most vase plants or bromeliads (pages 38-40) grow in the branches of trees in tropical forests. They have almost no roots and need very little material to grow in. They get most of their water from rain that falls in the "vase" formed by their leaves and most of their food from dead leaves that fall into the "vase" and rot.

To make a bromeliad tree, you will need a dead, but solid, branch of wood, cut to a convenient length. The more forks it has the more plants you can grow on it.

Fix the base of the branch to a board with Polyfilla. When it has set firm, put some stones on the board round the branch base for extra support.

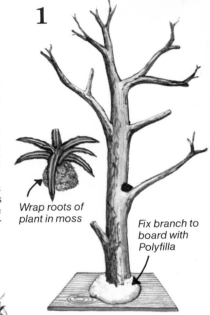

1

Wrap roots of plant in moss

Fix branch to board with Polyfilla

2

Stones

Take each plant and wrap its roots in sphagnum moss. Set each one into a fork of the branch, having first filled the fork with moist peat (fibrous peat is best). Wind some wire round the branch, the plant base and the moss. You may have to use a nail here and there to attach the wire more firmly.

Space the plants out, placing the larger ones near the base of the branch. Earth Stars usually grow in the ground and would look natural growing between the stones. Put the tree in a warm place near a window and keep the peat moist. Water the plants into their "vases" and give them a liquid feed occasionally.

Caring for indoor plants

Watering

Most plants should only be watered when the surface of the compost has become light brown in colour and feels dry and crumbly. Use soft water (boiled water is soft) which is at room temperature. Pour the water directly into the pot, filling the space between the rim of the pot and the surface of the compost. Pour it on fairly quickly and allow the water to drain away; plants should not stand in water. Plants that need moist compost at all times should be watered in the same way, but do so before the surface of the compost has dried out.

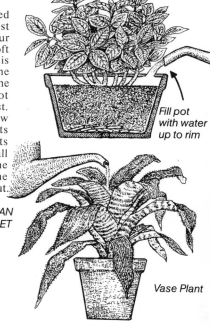

Fill pot with water up to rim

Vase Plant

AFRICAN VIOLET

Some plants, like the African Violet, need to be watered from below. To do this, stand the plant in a sink or bowl of water for about 20 minutes until the roots have absorbed the moisture they need.

Vase plants (bromeliads) should be watered directly into the vase formed by their leaves. Pour in soft water at room temperature until the vase is full. You should also keep the compost slightly moist.

Feeding

Potting compost contains quite a lot of plant food but plants will use up most of it after about a year, or even less if they are fast growers. You can provide the food that plants need with liquid or powder fertilizers, which you can buy in garden shops. Liquid fertilizers are concentrated mixtures and must be diluted with water. The powder ones can be put on dry, or mixed with water, depending on the brand. It is important to measure them exactly and give the plants the amount shown on the instructions on the container. Feed growing plants about once a week. Stop feeding when growth ceases, which for most indoor plants is in winter.

Providing humidity

When plants grow outdoors, they are in moist air and get rain on their leaves. The air in houses is usually dry, especially if there is central heating. Most plants, especially ferns, tend to wither indoors unless the air around them is kept fairly humid (moist). To provide plants with the humidity they need, you can spray their stems and leaves with water, using a mister. It is also a good idea to place several plants in a group together with a small dish of water in the middle. Water will then be constantly evaporating around them.

Mister

Water level should be below pot

Wet Peat

Plants that need a lot of humidity should be stood in a dish full of pebbles with a little water. Make sure that the water level is below the bottom of the pot, as plants do not do well if their roots are constantly soaked in water.

Another way to provide a lot of humidity for plants is to use peat. Place the plant in its pot inside another larger pot and pack wet peat into the space between them.

Grooming

To keep your plants looking their best, cut off withered or yellowing leaves and dead flowers. Keep the leaves clean and free of dust and dirt by wiping them with a clean, wet cloth or sponge. Do this every few weeks and the leaves of most plants will naturally have a healthy shine.

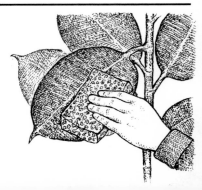

Training plants

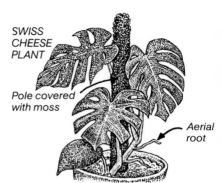

SWISS CHEESE PLANT

Pole covered with moss

Aerial root

Climbing plants need to be supported on a piece of trellis work or on a simple frame. You can make a simple frame with pieces of cane tied to one another with string. Other plants needing support can be attached to a piece of cane inserted in the compost. Tie the plant's stem loosely to the cane with string or wire.

Plants with aerial roots grow better if they are trained up a moss pole. You can buy a moss pole at a garden shop, or make one by binding sphagnum moss onto a stick with wire. If you attach the stem of a Swiss Cheese Plant to a moss pole, its aerial roots will grow into the moss. Keep the moss moist and the plant will thrive.

Choosing the right place

When you buy a plant, read the instructions that come with it, or check in this book, to see what light, humidity and warmth it needs.

Plants that need **good light** should be kept near a window and can be exposed to direct sunlight at all times except during the middle of the day in summer. At this time, the sun is too strong, except for a few plants such as cacti. Plants that need **indirect light** should be placed in a light place but never exposed to direct sunlight. Those which need **shade** should be kept away from windows.

Plants do not like extreme changes in temperature. If you keep plants on a window sill, bring them into the room on winter nights, as

▲ A kitchen window provides plants with good light as well as some humidity.

it will be too cold for them by the window. You can check the exact minimum temperature (MT) that each plant can survive, in this book. Never put plants in draughty places.

51

Repotting a plant

1

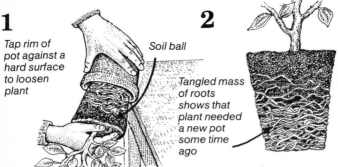

Tap rim of pot against a hard surface to loosen plant

Soil ball

2

Tangled mass of roots shows that plant needed a new pot some time ago

As plants grow, they need fresh compost and larger pots. To tell if a plant needs repotting, take it out of its pot. To do this, turn the plant in its pot upside down so that it rests on the palm of your hand. Hold the pot with the other hand and bang the rim against a hard surface. The soil ball will fall complete into your hand.

If the roots are wound round and round the outside of the compost, the plant needs repotting. If you cannot tip a plant out of its pot because it is too large, look at the bottom to see if roots are growing out through the drainage hole. Another sign that repotting is necessary is the appearance of roots above the top of the compost.

3

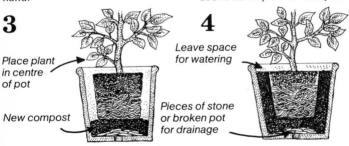

Place plant in centre of pot

New compost

4

Leave space for watering

Pieces of stone or broken pot for drainage

Take a pot one size larger than the plant's old pot (usually about two and a half centimetres wider across). Place a few stones, or pieces of broken pot, over the drainage hole to stop it becoming blocked. Then put in a little fresh compost, which you can buy from a garden shop, and place the soil bail of the plant in the centre of the pot.

Hold the plant with one hand while you put compost in the space between the soil ball and pot with the other. Firm it down gently with your fingers. You should leave a space of two to five centimetres between the rim of the pot and the compost for watering. Water the plant well and put it in a warm, shady place for a few days to recover.

Growing new plants

SPIDER PLANT

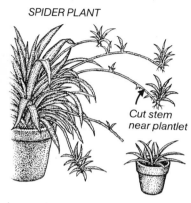

Cut stem near plantlet

Spider Plant

There are several different ways to start new plants from ones that you already have. Some of the easiest plants to start new ones from are those that produce plantlets, like the Spider Plant. The plantlets form at the end of a stem and are complete with roots. When the roots are about one and a half centimetres long, cut the stem close to the plantlet and put it into a five-centimetre pot of compost so that the roots are fully covered.

Wandering Jew

New plants can also be started from the stems of some plants like Wandering Jew (Tradescantia). To do this, cut a piece, about ten centimetres long, from the end of a stem just below a leaf or pair of leaves. Then cut off the bottom leaves, put the stem into a glass of water and place it in a warm position. After about eight days, roots will start to grow and you can then plant the stem in a pot of special compost for cuttings.

Instead of putting the cutting into water, you can put it directly into moist compost at the side of a five-centimetre pot. Cover the pot with a clear, blown-up polythene bag and fasten this round the pot with an elastic band or piece of string. Put it in a warm shady place and after about a week, take the bag off and gently pull the cutting. If it has rooted, it will feel quite firm and will not come out of the compost. You can then leave the bag off and treat it as a normal plant.

Cut here

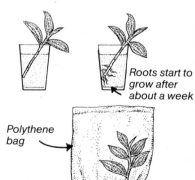

Roots start to grow after about a week

Polythene bag

Plant problems

If a plant is not growing as well as usual, or begins to look unhealthy, it is most likely due to one of the following points:

● Not enough water
● Too much water
● Not enough food
● Pot is too small
● Not enough light or warmth
● Too much exposure to sunlight
● Sudden change in conditions
● Air is too dry

Pests and diseases are not usually a problem on indoor plants, but you may occasionally find greenfly or scale insects. Scale insects look like small brown spots and appear underneath leaves and on stems. If you find greenfly or scale insects, rub them off with your finger nail.

Below is a list of the most common problems with indoor plants and what causes them.

Tips and edges of leaves turn brown. *Not enough humidity or plant has been watered with hard water.*

Plant wilts and leaves droop. *Not enough water or, in some cases, too much water. If flowers and flower buds drop, the problem could be lack of water or humidity, or a sudden change of temperature.*

Healthy leaf

Stem and leaves turn pale green. *Not enough light or a lack of food. If leaves that are normally coloured lose their colour and turn plain green, the plant may not have enough light.*

Leaves turn yellow. *This can be due to over-watering, or lack of warmth, or to draughts.*

Leaves fall off plant. *Plants naturally lose one or two lower leaves each year, but if many leaves suddenly fall off, the plant has probably had a sudden change in growing conditions, for example, too much warmth all of a sudden.*

Plant does not grow or grows more slowly than usual. *This is normal in winter, but in summer it may mean that the plant needs a larger pot or more fresh compost.*

Growing plants from pips

It is quite easy to grow indoor plants from pips and stones, and from tree seeds that you find in autumn. Plant several pips or seeds at a time, as not all will germinate to form new plants.

Oranges and lemons

Orange tree

To start an orange or lemon tree, put some seed compost in a small container, such as a yoghurt pot. Put in several pips and just cover them with a layer of compost. Keep the compost moist and put the pot in a warm, dark place. When shoots appear, bring the pot into the light. When the shoots are about five centimetres, pick out the strongest ones and plant in separate pots.

Tree seedlings

Horse Chestnut tree grown from a conker

Collect tree seeds, such as acorns and conkers, in autumn, and plant them in compost in individual pots. Leave the pots outside over winter, covered with net to keep mice away. If the seeds did not sprout the previous autumn, they will do so in spring. They grow quickly and soon need a larger pot. You could plant them in the garden. Be careful not to damage the main root.

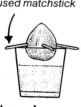

Toothpick or used matchstick

Pinch out top shoot when plant has four or five leaves

Plant in compost when roots are well formed

Avocados

To start an avocado plant, fix three used matchsticks or toothpicks into an avocado stone. Place it over a jar of water, so that the base of the stone is just above the water. After a few weeks, the stone will split and a stem and roots start to grow.

When they are well formed, plant the stone in compost in a ten-centimetre pot, but do not quite cover the top of the stone. To stop the plant growing too tall, break off the tip of the shoot just above a leaf. This will encourage branches to grow out lower down the stem.

Making a bottle garden

Instead of growing a plant on its own in a pot, you could try growing several plants together in a large glass bottle or an old goldfish bowl. Plants grown in this way create their own moist atmosphere and need little watering. The type of plants to grow are those needing a humid atmosphere, mostly the small, leafy kinds such as the Earth-stars, the small-leaved variegated ivies, the Snakeskin Plant, *Pilea cadierei nana*, *Pilea spruceana*, *Peperomia caperata,* the Marantas, Maidenhair Fern, and the Piggy-back Plant. You can grow between three to seven plants together, depending on the size of the jar or bottle you use.

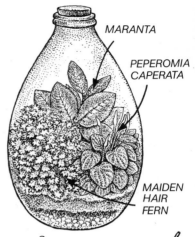

MARANTA

PEPEROMIA CAPERATA

MAIDEN HAIR FERN

Jars and Tools

Goldfish bowl

Storage jar

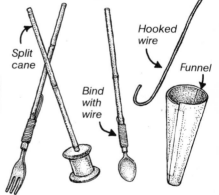

Split cane

Bind with wire

Hooked wire

Funnel

You can use any large glass jar or bowl to plant your garden in, but it should have a stopper, such as a cork. If it does not, you can cover the opening with a piece of polystyrene.

To make your bottle garden, you will need some small tools with long handles, which you can make yourself. With some string or wire, bind the handles of an old fork and a tablespoon to split canes so that they are long enough to reach inside the bottle. Fix a cotton reel to another piece of cane, and get a piece of wire and bend the end into a hook. Make a long funnel from a piece of stiff paper.

Preparing the bottle

To prepare the bottle for planting you will need some potting compost, some small pebbles, charcoal (which you can get from an artists' supplies shop or a garden shop) and a jugful of soft (boiled) water at room temperature. First clean the bottle, then pour the pebbles into it using the funnel. They should form a layer about three centimetres deep. You can make the surface level by tapping it with the cotton reel. Now add a layer of charcoal, in the same way, about one centimetre deep. Finally add the compost, tapping it down to form a layer about five centimetres deep.

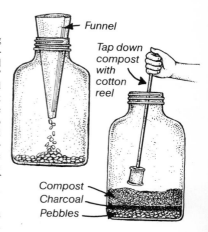

Funnel

Tap down compost with cotton reel

Compost
Charcoal
Pebbles

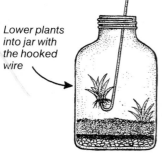

Lower plants into jar with the hooked wire

Planting

Make a shallow hole in the compost at one side of the bottle with the fork and then, using the hooked wire, lower a plant into the bottle. Use the spoon to cover the roots with compost. Continue to add plants round the edges of the bottle and plant the centre last. Make sure the plants are firmly embedded in the compost and try not to dirty the sides of the bottle as you lower in the plants.

Watering

When you have put the plants in the bottle, pour a little water into the compost. Put the stopper on the bottle and place it in a shaded place for a few days.

If the moisture content inside the bottle is right, condensation will appear on the sides in the morning and disappear during the day. If there is no condensation, you need to add a little water. If there is condensation all the time, take the stopper off for a day or two to allow the bottle to dry out.

Drops of moisture should only be present in the mornings

Sprouting seeds

Mustard and cress

The mustard and cress sold by greengrocers for salads are grown from seeds. You can buy these from a garden shop and grow your own quite easily at home. To do this, place some wet cotton wool on a saucer or in an empty egg shell. Press the seeds down into the cotton wool and put them in a warm, dark place. If you want the cress and mustard to be ready to eat at the same time, sow the cress first and the mustard three days later. If the cotton wool dries out add some more water.

When the seeds start to sprout, bring them into the light. After a week, both mustard and cress will have grown about five centimetres high and will be ready to eat.

MUSTARD — CRESS

Saucer — Damp cotton wool

You could paint a face on the egg shell

Bean sprouts

There are many kinds of seeds, beans and grains from which you can grow sprouts to eat. The bean sprouts used in Chinese cooking are grown from mung beans. They can be bought in garden and whole-food shops. To grow the sprouts, you will need a large glass jar, a square of muslin and an elastic band.

Put some mung beans in the jar and fill it with tepid water. Secure the muslin over the opening with the rubber band and place the jar in a warm, dark place for six hours. Then pour off the water through the muslin, rinse the beans with fresh water and drain them again. Put the jar back in a dark place. Rinse and drain the beans every morning and evening until the sprouts are about five centimetres long, when they will be ready to eat. You could also try sprouting other beans in the same way.

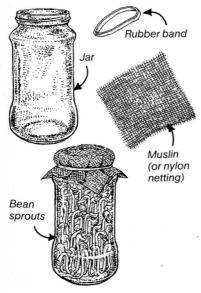

Rubber band

Jar

Muslin (or nylon netting)

Bean sprouts

Books to read

Dictionary of Indoor plants in Colour. R. Hay, F. R. McQuown & G. & K. Beckett (Ebury Press & Michael Joseph). This book has lots of good colour photographs, and is useful for looking up the names of indoor plants.

Be Your Own Houseplant Expert. D. G. Hessayon (PBI) is a cheap and helpful guide about the general care of indoor plants.

Mr Smith's Indoor Garden. Geoffrey Smith (BBC) is a cheap paperback, packed with information.

Houseplants in Colour. Rob Herwig (David & Charles) has good photographs of many plants and information on how to care for them.

The Best of Houseplants. Suzanne Mitchell (Hamlyn). Another useful book on identification and care of plants.

The Pip Book. K. Mossman (Penguin) is a cheap, practical paperback, and tells you how to grow all sorts of plants from pips, stones, pineapple tops and so on.

Clubs to join

There are houseplant societies that you can join if you want to learn more about indoor plants and how to look after them. Some national societies have local branches, and some do not. Some are specialist and concerned only with, for example, cacti or bromeliads; others deal with the whole range of indoor plants. Here are the addresses of a few clubs should you wish to write to the secretaries for further details (remember to send a stamped addressed envelope for their reply):

The Saintpaulia and Houseplant Society (Sec. Miss N. Tanburn, 82, Rossmore Court, Park Road, London NW1) has about 500 members. There are no branches, but the society runs monthly and annual meetings and competitions. It also gives advice, has a library which members can use and organizes the exchange of plant material.

The National Cactus and Succulent Society (Sec. Mr J. W. P. Mullard, 19, Crabtree Road, Botley, Oxford OX2 9DU) has 105 branches around the country which hold monthly meetings and lectures. Juniors (under 18) and O.A.P.s pay reduced subscription.

The British Bromeliad Society (Sec. Mr R. Lucibell, Dept. of Botany, Queen Mary College, Mile End Road, London E1) are a specialist society with about 250 members.

The Cactus and Succulent Society of Great Britain (Write to: Mrs B. Maddams, 26, Glenfield Road, Banstead, Surrey) may have a branch near you. They hold lectures and shows, and offer reduced rates to juniors (under 16).

If you get really interested in indoor plants, you could form your own society with friends, and organize talks and shows, and exchange plants and cuttings.

Scorecard

The plants in this scorecard are arranged in alphabetical order. When you spot a plant, fill in the date next to its name. You can add up your score after a day out spotting.

	Score	Date seen		Score	Date seen
African Violet	5		Calamondin Orange	15	
Aluminium Plant	5		Calathea ornata	20	
Amaryllis	15		Cape Primrose	25	
Asparagus Fern	15		Cherry, Christmas	5	
Asparagus sprengeri	10		Cherry, Jerusalem	15	
Azalea	5		Chinese Evergreen	5	
Bead Plant	20		Chinese Evergreen, 'Silver Queen'	15	
Begonia, Double-flowered	10		Chinese Rose	20	
Begonia, 'Fireglow'	15		Christmas Pepper	5	
Begonia, Iron Cross	15		Cleistocactus strausii	15	
Begonia, Multicoloured	5		Clog Plant	20	
Begonia, Purple-leaved	5		Cordyline	10	
Billbergia	20		Crocus	5	
Busy Lizzie	5		Croton	10	
Cactus, Christmas	10		Crown of Thorns	20	
Cactus, Column	15		Cyclamen	5	
Cactus, Easter	15		Daffodil	5	
Cactus, Old Man	15		Devil's Ivy	10	
Cactus, Orchid	15		Devil's Ivy, White	15	
Cactus, Peanut	15		Dipladenia splendens	20	
Caladium	25		Dracaena fragrans massangeana	15	

	Score	Date seen		Score	Date seen
Dracaena godseffiana	10		Italian Bellflower	15	
Dracaena sanderiana	10		Ivy, Arrow-leaved	10	
Dracaena, Three-coloured	20		Ivy, 'Goldheart'	10	
Dracaena, 'Victoriae'	20		Ivy, 'Lutzii'	10	
Dumb Cane	5		Ivy, Variegated Canary	5	
Earth Star	15		Joseph's Coat	5	
False Aralia	20		Kalanchoe	10	
Fern, Cristate Ribbon	15		Kangaroo Vine	5	
Fern, Maidenhair	10		Lily, Boat	15	
Fern, Stag's Horn	20		Lily, Kaffir	20	
Fern, Sword	10		Lily, Peace	20	
Fern, Variegated Ribbon	20		Living Stones	20	
Fig, Mistletoe	15		Lollipop Plant	10	
Fig, Trailing	20		Mammillaria	15	
Fig, Weeping	15		Maranta, Three-coloured	20	
Fittonia verschaffeltii	20		Mother-in-law's Tongue	5	
Flamingo Flower	25		Neoregelia 'Tricolor'	15	
Geranium	5		Norfolk Island Pine	15	
Gloxinia	15		Palm, Date	20	
Golden Bird's Nest	20		Palm, Kentia	10	
Grape Ivy	5		Palm, Parlour	10	
Guzmania	20		Partridge-breasted Aloe	20	
Gymnocalycium 'Ruby Ball'	25		Peperomia argyreia	15	
Houseleek	20		Peperomia caperata	5	
Hyacinth	5		Peperomia 'Greengold'	15	

	Score	Date seen		Score	Date seen
Pineapple, Variegated	25		Starfish Plant	20	
Philodendron bipinnatifidum	20		String of Hearts	20	
Piggy-back Plant	20		Sundew	20	
Pilea involucrata	10		Sweetheart Vine	5	
Pilea 'Moonglow'	15		Swiss Cheese Plant	10	
Poinsettia	5		Tillandsia cyanea	25	
Prayer Plant	10		Umbrella Plant	20	
Prickly Pear	15		Urn Plant	10	
Purple Heart	20		Venus Fly-trap	20	
Purple Passion Vine	25		Vriesea 'Flaming Sword'	15	
Rhoicissus 'Ellen Danica'	10		Wandering Jew, Coloured	5	
Rubber Plant	5		Wandering Jew, Large	15	
Schefflera actinophylla	20		Wandering Jew, Yellow	10	
Shrimp Plant	10		Wax Flower	15	
Snakeskin Plant	10		Zebra Plant	5	
Spider Plant	5		Zebrina pendula	10	
Spotted Dog	15				

Index

The Scientific name of each plant is written in brackets after its common name.